desserts

simple and delicious easy-to-make recipes

Lorraine Turner

p

This is a Parragon Publishing Book
First published in 2002

Parragon Publishing
Queen Street House
4 Queen Street
Bath, BA1 1HE, UK

ISBN: 0-75258-869-9

Printed in China

Produced by the Bridgewater Book Company Ltd.

Photographer Calvey Taylor-Haw

Home Economist Ruth Pollock

NOTES FOR THE READER

- This book uses both imperial and metric measurements. Follow the same units of measurement throughout; do not mix imperial and metric.

- All spoon measurements are level: teaspoons are assumed to be 5 ml, and tablespoons are assumed to be 15 ml.

- Unless otherwise stated, milk is assumed to be whole milk, eggs and individual vegetables such as potatoes are medium, and pepper is freshly ground black pepper.

- Recipes using raw or very lightly cooked eggs should be avoided by infants, the elderly, pregnant women, convalescents, and anyone suffering from an illness.

- The times given are an approximate guide only. Preparation times differ according to the techniques used by different people and the cooking times may also vary from those given. Optional ingredients, variations, or serving suggestions have not been included in the calculations.

contents

introduction   4

sponges, bakes & cakes   6

pies & tarts   28

hot desserts   46

cold desserts   68

index   96

introduction

There is nothing quite like a dessert to round off a meal. A successful dessert is always irresistible, and the ever-widening range of delicious ingredients available nowadays has brought newer and even more exciting flavors to our tables.

This book is bursting with delicious recipes. You will recognize some traditional favorites, such as Sticky Toffee Sponge, Banoffee Pie, Bakewell Tart, and Apricot Crumble. There is also a tempting selection of contemporary and international dishes for you to try, such as Rose Petal Ice Cream or Toffee Bananas. Chocolate-lovers will be unable to resist the Chocolate Cherry Layer Cake and the Rich Chocolate Mousses, and the health-conscious among you will enjoy some of the fruit desserts or lighter concoctions such as Summer Pudding, Baked Peaches with Orange Liqueur Cream, and the Peach & Banana Sherbet.

All the recipes in this book are accompanied by lavish full-color photographs and clear, step-by-step instructions, to ensure perfect desserts every time. So whether you are catering for a large dinner party, a few family members, or just for yourself, there will be something in this book to suit every occasion and every taste.

guide to recipe key		
	very easy	Recipes are graded as follows: 1 pea = easy; 2 peas = very easy; 3 peas = extremely easy.
	serves 4	Recipes generally serve four people. Simply halve the ingredients to serve two, taking care not to mix imperial and metric measurements.
	10 minutes	Preparation time. Where marinating or soaking are involved, these times have been added on separately: eg, 15 minutes + 30 minutes to marinate.
	10 minutes	Cooking time. Cooking times do not include the cooking of side dishes or accompaniments served with the main dishes.

hot syrup sponge
page 12

peach and strawberry tart
page 42

stuffed pears
page 54

cherry baskets
page 80

sponges, bakes & cakes

Where would we be without comforting, hot sponge desserts and tempting cakes? The recipes in this chapter are a feast for the senses and the taste buds. From Individual Chocolate Desserts and Creamy Rice to Apple Upside-Down Cake and Roly Poly Pudding, these dishes are easy to prepare and a delight to cook. They are full of irresistible ingredients and rich flavors, and provide a satisfying treat in themselves or a marvelous finish to any meal.

sticky toffee sponge

		ingredients	
very easy		SPONGE	STICKY TOFFEE SAUCE
		scant ½ cup golden raisins	2 tbsp butter
serves 4		generous ¾ cup stoned dates, chopped	¾ cup heavy cream
		1 tsp baking soda	1 cup brown sugar
		2 tbsp butter, plus extra for greasing	
10–15 minutes		1 cup brown sugar	grated orange zest, to decorate
		2 eggs	freshly whipped cream, to serve
		scant 1½ cups self-rising flour, sifted	
35–40 minutes			

To make the sponge, put the fruits and baking soda into a heatproof bowl. Cover with boiling water and set aside to soak.

Preheat the oven to 350°F/180°C. Grease a round cake pan, 8 inches/20 cm in diameter, with butter. Put the remaining butter in a separate bowl, add the sugar, and mix well. Beat in the eggs then fold in the flour. Drain the soaked fruits, add to the bowl, and mix. Spoon the mixture evenly into the prepared cake pan. Transfer to the preheated oven and bake for 35–40 minutes. The sponge is cooked when a skewer inserted into the center comes out clean. About 5 minutes before the end of the cooking time, make the sauce. Melt the butter in a pan over medium heat. Stir in the cream and sugar and bring to a boil, stirring constantly. Lower the heat and simmer for 5 minutes.

Turn out the sponge onto a serving plate and pour over the sauce. Decorate with grated orange zest and serve with whipped cream.

individual chocolate desserts

		ingredients	
easy		**DESSERTS**	**CHOCOLATE SAUCE**
serves 4		$\frac{1}{2}$ cup superfine sugar 3 eggs $\frac{1}{2}$ cup all-purpose flour	2 tbsp unsalted butter $3\frac{1}{2}$ oz/100 g semisweet chocolate 5 tbsp water
10–15 minutes		$\frac{1}{2}$ cup unsweetened cocoa scant $\frac{1}{2}$ cup unsalted butter, melted, plus extra for greasing $3\frac{1}{2}$ oz/100 g semisweet chocolate, melted	1 tbsp superfine sugar 1 tbsp coffee-flavored liqueur, such as Kahlua coffee beans, to decorate
50 minutes			

To make the desserts, put the sugar and eggs into a heatproof bowl and place over a pan of simmering water. Whisk for about 10 minutes until frothy. Remove the bowl from the heat and fold in the flour and cocoa. Fold in the butter, then the chocolate. Mix well. Grease 4 small heatproof bowls with butter. Spoon the mixture into the bowls and cover with waxed paper. Top with foil and secure with string. Place the desserts in a large pan filled with enough simmering water to reach halfway up the sides of the bowls. Steam for about 40 minutes, or until cooked through.

About 2–3 minutes before the end of the cooking time, make the sauce. Put the butter, chocolate, water, and sugar into a small pan and warm over low heat, stirring constantly, until melted together. Stir in the liqueur.

Remove the desserts from the heat, turn out into serving dishes, and pour over the sauce. Decorate with coffee beans and serve.

hot syrup sponge

very easy	**ingredients**	
	3 tbsp butter, plus extra for greasing	1 tsp vanilla extract
	2 tbsp superfine sugar	4 tbsp corn syrup
serves 4–6	2 eggs	
	6 tbsp all-purpose flour	thin strips of candied orange peel,
	1 tsp baking powder	to decorate
10–15 minutes	6 tbsp milk	hot custard, to serve
1½ hours		

Lightly grease a large heatproof bowl with butter. Put the remaining butter into a separate bowl with the sugar, and cream together until fluffy. Add the eggs and beat together well. Mix in the flour and baking powder, then stir in the milk and vanilla extract. Continue to stir until smooth.

Pour the corn syrup into the prepared heatproof bowl, then spoon the dessert mixture on top. Cover with waxed paper and top with a piece of aluminum foil, tied on securely with string. Transfer to a large pan filled with enough simmering water to reach halfway up the sides of the heatproof bowl. Simmer gently for about 1½ hours until cooked right through, topping up the water level when necessary.

Lift out the bowl and let rest for 5 minutes, then turn the sponge out onto a serving plate. Decorate with thin strips of candied orange peel and serve hot, with custard.

roly poly pudding

		ingredients	
easy		1¼ cups self-rising flour, plus extra for dusting	2 tbsp milk
		pinch of salt	1 tbsp butter, for greasing
serves 4		2¾ oz/75 g shredded suet	raspberries, to decorate
		3–4 tbsp hot water	
20 minutes		6 tbsp raspberry preserve	custard, to serve
1½ hours			

Put the flour and salt into a bowl and mix together well. Add the suet, then stir in enough hot water to make a light dough. Using your hands, shape the dough into a ball. Turn out the dough onto a lightly floured counter and knead gently until smooth. Roll out into a rectangle about 11 inches/28 cm x 9 inches/23 cm.

Spread the raspberry preserve over the dough, leaving a border of about ½ inch/1 cm all round. Brush the border with milk. Starting with the short side, roll up the dough evenly into one large roll.

Lightly grease a large piece of aluminum foil with butter, then place the dough roll in the center. Gently close up the foil around the dough, allowing room for expansion, and seal tightly. Transfer to a steamer on top of a pan of boiling water. Steam for about 1½ hours until cooked, topping up the water level when necessary.

Turn out the roly poly onto a serving platter and decorate with raspberries. Serve with hot custard.

creamy rice dessert

		ingredients	
	very easy	1 tbsp butter, for greasing	1 tsp vanilla extract
		½ cup golden raisins	finely grated zest of 1 large lemon
	serves 4	5 tbsp superfine sugar	pinch of nutmeg
		3¼ oz/90 g sweet rice	
		5 cups milk	chopped pistachios, to decorate
	10–15 minutes		
	2½ hours		

Preheat the oven to 325°F/160°C. Grease a 3½-cup ovenproof dish with butter.

Put the golden raisins, sugar, and rice into a mixing bowl, then stir in the milk and vanilla extract. Transfer to the prepared dish, sprinkle over the grated lemon zest and the nutmeg, then bake in the preheated oven for 2½ hours.

Remove from the oven and transfer to individual serving bowls. Decorate with chopped pistachios and serve.

eve's apple bake

		ingredients
very easy	scant ½ cup butter	1½ tbsp currants
	1 lb 2 oz/500 g cooking apples, peeled	1 egg, beaten
serves 4	and cored	generous 1 cup self-rising flour
	1 tbsp lemon juice	2–3 tbsp milk
	¾ cup superfine sugar	
15 minutes	1 tsp ground allspice	chopped mixed nuts, to decorate
	¼ cup golden raisins	heavy cream, to serve
45 minutes		

Preheat the oven to 350°F/180°C. Grease a 3½-cup ovenproof dish with a little butter.

Slice the cooking apples and put them into a bowl with the lemon juice. Stir the apples gently to coat them in the lemon juice. Sprinkle over half of the sugar, then add the allspice, golden raisins, and currants. Mix together well, then spoon the mixture into the prepared ovenproof dish.

In a separate bowl, cream together the remaining butter and sugar, then gradually mix in the beaten egg. Fold in the flour, then stir in enough milk to give the mixture a light, dropping consistency. Transfer to the ovenproof dish and spread evenly over the fruit. Scatter over the chopped nuts and bake in the preheated oven for 45 minutes until golden.

Remove from the oven and serve hot with heavy cream.

summer pudding

	ingredients	
easy	7 oz/200 g strawberries, hulled and quartered	1 tsp ground allspice
	7 oz/200 g blueberries	8 medium slices of day-old white bread, crusts removed
serves 4–6	7 oz/200 g raspberries	
	7 oz/200 g cranberries	whole strawberries, blueberries, raspberries, cranberries, and blackberries, to decorate
	7 oz/200 g blackberries	
20 minutes + 2–8 hours to chill	6 tbsp superfine sugar	
	2 tbsp lemon juice	heavy cream, to serve (optional)
	2 tbsp sherry	
5 minutes		

Put the fruit into a pan over medium heat. Stir in the sugar, lemon juice, sherry, and allspice. Heat for 5 minutes until the sugar has dissolved. Remove from the heat and let cool.

Cut the bread diagonally into fourths, then use it to line the bottom and sides of a 3½-cup bowl, keeping a few pieces to one side (you may need to trim some of the pieces to fit). Spoon the cooled berry mixture into the prepared bowl and cover with the remaining bread. Place the bowl inside another, shallower bowl to catch any overflowing juices, then top with a plate that fits snugly inside its rim. Place a can of food on top to weigh the plate down, then refrigerate for at least 2 hours, but preferably overnight.

To serve, remove the can and plate, loosen the sides of the summer pudding with a knife, then turn out onto a serving plate. Decorate with berries and serve with heavy cream, if using.

bread & butter dessert

		ingredients
very easy		6 medium slices of day-old whole-wheat bread, crusts removed 1½ tbsp currants
serves 4		generous 1¾ cups milk
15 minutes		
40 minutes		

ingredients

6 medium slices of day-old whole-
  wheat bread, crusts removed
2 tbsp butter
2 tbsp sugar
1 tbsp golden raisins

1½ tbsp currants
generous 1¾ cups milk
2 eggs
½ tsp ground allspice

Preheat the oven to 350°F/180°C. Spread the slices of bread with
butter, then cut each slice into fourths. Arrange half of the bread,
buttered side up, on the bottom of a 3½-cup ovenproof dish.
Sprinkle over half of the sugar, then scatter over half of the golden
raisins and currants. Top with the remaining bread, then sprinkle
over the remaining sugar and fruit.

Pour the milk into a large mixing bowl. Add the eggs and allspice
and whisk until smooth. Pour the mixture evenly over the bread,
then transfer to the preheated oven and bake for about
40 minutes. Remove from the oven and serve hot.

apple upside-down cake

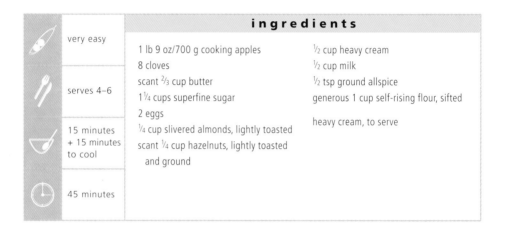

	ingredients
very easy	1 lb 9 oz/700 g cooking apples ½ cup heavy cream

ingredients

very easy

serves 4–6

15 minutes
+ 15 minutes
to cool

45 minutes

1 lb 9 oz/700 g cooking apples
8 cloves
scant ⅔ cup butter
1¼ cups superfine sugar
2 eggs
¼ cup slivered almonds, lightly toasted
scant ¼ cup hazelnuts, lightly toasted
   and ground

½ cup heavy cream
½ cup milk
½ tsp ground allspice
generous 1 cup self-rising flour, sifted

heavy cream, to serve

Preheat the oven to 350°F/180°C. Bring a large pan of water to a boil. Peel and core the apples, cut into slices, then add them to the pan with the cloves. Lower the heat and simmer for 5 minutes, then remove from the heat. Drain well. Discard the cloves. Let the apple cool a little.

Grease an 8-inch/20-cm diameter cake pan with butter. Arrange the cooked apple slices over the bottom of the pan and sprinkle over 2 tablespoons of the sugar. In a separate bowl, cream together the remaining butter and sugar. Gradually mix in the eggs, then the nuts, cream, milk, and allspice. Gradually beat in the flour until smooth. Spread the mixture evenly over the apples, then bake the cake in the preheated oven for about 40 minutes, until golden. The cake is cooked when a skewer inserted into the center comes out clean. Remove from the oven and let cool for 5 minutes, then turn out onto a serving plate. Serve with cream.

chocolate cherry layer cake

		ingredients	
easy		3 tbsp unsalted butter, melted, plus extra for greasing	½ tsp baking powder 4 eggs
makes one 9-inch/23-cm cake		2 lb/900 g fresh cherries, pitted and halved generous 1¼ cups superfine sugar	4 cups heavy cream DECORATION
15 minutes + 30 minutes to cool		scant ½ cup cherry brandy ¾ cup all-purpose flour ½ cup unsweetened cocoa	grated semisweet chocolate whole fresh cherries
50–55 minutes			

Preheat the oven to 350°F/180°C. Grease and line a 9-inch/23-cm springform cake pan. Put the halved cherries into a pan, add 3 tablespoons of the sugar and the cherry brandy. Simmer for 5 minutes. Drain, reserving the syrup. In another bowl, sift together the flour, cocoa, and baking powder.

Put the eggs in a heatproof bowl and beat in a generous ¾ cup of the sugar. Place the bowl over a pan of simmering water and beat for 6 minutes until thickened. Remove from the heat, then gradually fold in the flour mixture and melted butter. Spoon into the cake pan. Bake for 40 minutes. Remove from the oven and let cool. Turn out the cake and cut in half horizontally. Mix the cream with the remaining sugar. Spread the reserved syrup over the cut sides of the cake. Arrange the cherries over one half, top with a layer of cream, and place the other half on top. Cover with cream, press grated chocolate all over, and decorate with cherries.

pies
& tarts

What can be more enticing than a flood of sweet fruits cascading from a warm pie, or a succulent tart studded with fruits and laced with spices? The stunning display of pies and tarts in this chapter will have every member of the household asking for more, and every dinner guest longing to be offered another piece. From the Forest Fruit Pie to the Chocolate Orange Tart, the only problem you will have with these recipes is that as soon as the serving plate is empty, your diners will want more.

forest fruit pie

ingredients

easy	

9 oz/250 g blueberries
9 oz/250 g raspberries
9 oz/250 g blackberries
$\frac{1}{2}$ cup superfine sugar
scant 1 $\frac{1}{2}$ cups all-purpose flour, plus
  extra for dusting
scant $\frac{1}{4}$ cup ground hazelnuts
scant $\frac{1}{2}$ cup butter, diced, plus extra
  for greasing

finely grated zest of 1 lemon
1 egg yolk, beaten
4 tbsp milk

2 tsp confectioner's sugar, to dust

whipped cream, to serve

easy

serves 4

**20 minutes
+ 30 minutes
to rest**

45 minutes

Put the fruit into a pan with 3 tablespoons of superfine sugar and simmer, stirring, for 5 minutes. Remove from the heat. Sift the flour into a bowl, then add the hazelnuts. Rub in the butter, then sift in the remaining sugar. Add the lemon zest, egg yolk, and 3 tablespoons of milk, and mix. Turn out onto a lightly floured counter and knead briefly. Let rest for 30 minutes.

Preheat the oven to 375°F/190°C. Grease an 8-inch/20-cm ovenproof pie dish with butter. Roll out half the dough to a thickness of $\frac{1}{4}$ inch/5 mm and use it to line the dish. Spoon the fruit into the pie shell. Brush the rim with water, then roll out the remaining dough and use it to cover the pie. Trim and crimp the edges, make 2 small slits in the top, and decorate with 2 leaf shapes cut from the dough trimmings. Brush all over with the remaining milk. Bake for 40 minutes. Remove from the oven, sprinkle over the confectioner's sugar, and serve with whipped cream.

banoffee pie

		ingredients	
easy		two cans sweetened condensed milk, about 14 fl oz/400 ml each	4 ripe bananas
			1 tbsp lemon juice
serves 4		6 tbsp butter, melted	1 tsp vanilla extract
		5½ oz/150 g graham crackers, crushed into crumbs	2¾ oz/75 g chocolate, grated
20 minutes + 1 hour to cool		⅓ cup almonds, toasted and ground	scant 2 cups thick heavy cream, whipped
2¼ hours		⅓ cup hazelnuts, toasted and ground	

Place the cans of milk in a large pan and cover them with water. Bring to a boil, then reduce the heat and simmer for 2 hours, topping up the water level regularly to keep the cans covered. Carefully lift out the hot cans and let cool.

Preheat the oven to 350°F/180°C. Grease a 9-inch/23-cm tart pan with butter. Put the remaining butter into a bowl and add the crackers and nuts. Mix together well, then press the mixture evenly into the bottom and sides of the tart pan. Bake for 10–12 minutes, then remove from the oven and let cool.

Peel and slice the bananas and put them into a bowl. Sprinkle over the lemon juice and vanilla extract and mix gently. Spread the banana mixture over the cracker layer in the pan, then open the cans of condensed milk and spoon the contents over the bananas. Sprinkle over 1¾ oz/50 g of the chocolate, then top with a thick layer of whipped cream. Scatter over the remaining chocolate and serve.

lemon meringue pie

		ingredients
easy		

easy	
serves 4	
20 minutes + 30 minutes to rest	
1 hour	

ingredients

PIE DOUGH
scant 1½ cups all-purpose flour, plus
  extra for dusting
scant ½ cup butter, diced, plus extra
  for greasing
scant ½ cup confectioner's
  sugar, sifted
finely grated zest of 1 lemon
1 egg yolk, beaten
3 tbsp milk

FILLING
3 tbsp cornstarch
1¼ cups cold water
juice and grated zest of 2 lemons
scant 1 cup superfine sugar
2 eggs, separated

To make the pie dough, sift the flour into a bowl and rub in the butter. Mix in the remaining ingredients. Knead briefly on a lightly floured counter. Let rest for 30 minutes. Preheat the oven to 350°F/180°C. Grease an 8-inch/20-cm ovenproof pie dish with butter. Roll out the dough to a thickness of ¼ inch/5 mm and use it to line the dish. Prick with a fork, line with baking parchment, and fill with baking beans. Bake for 15 minutes. Remove from the oven. Lower the temperature to 300°F/150°C.

To make the filling, mix the cornstarch with a little water. Put the remaining water into a pan. Stir in the lemon juice and zest and cornstarch paste. Bring to a boil, stirring. Cook for 2 minutes. Cool a little. Stir in 5 tablespoons of sugar and the egg yolks, and pour into the tart shell. In a separate bowl, whisk the egg whites until stiff. Gradually whisk in the remaining sugar and spread over the pie. Bake for 40 minutes. Remove from the oven and serve.

bakewell tart

		ingredients	
easy		**PIE DOUGH**	**FILLING**
serves 4		scant 1½ cups all-purpose flour, plus extra for dusting	scant ½ cup butter
			½ cup brown sugar
		scant ½ cup butter, diced, plus extra for greasing	2 eggs, beaten
20 minutes + 30 minutes to rest			1 tsp almond extract
		scant ½ cup confectioner's sugar, sifted	75 g/2¾ oz ground rice
			3 tbsp ground almonds
		finely grated zest of 1 lemon	3 tbsp slivered almonds, toasted
40 minutes		1 egg yolk, beaten	
		3 tbsp milk	confectioner's sugar, to dust
		4 tbsp strawberry preserve	

To make the pie dough, sift the flour into a bowl. Rub in the butter. Mix in the confectioner's sugar, lemon zest, egg yolk, and milk. Knead briefly on a lightly floured counter. Let rest for 30 minutes.

Preheat the oven to 375°F/190°C. Grease an 8-inch/20-cm ovenproof tart pan with butter. Roll out the dough to a thickness of ¼ inch/5 mm and use it to line the bottom and sides of the pan. Prick all over the bottom with a fork, then spread with preserve.

To make the filling, cream together the butter and sugar until fluffy. Gradually beat in the eggs, followed by the almond extract, ground rice, and ground almonds. Spread the mixture evenly over the preserve-covered tart shell, then scatter over the slivered almonds. Bake in the preheated oven for 40 minutes, until golden. Remove from the oven, dust with confectioner's sugar, and serve.

chocolate orange tart

		ingredients	
easy		**PIE DOUGH**	**FILLING & ORANGE CREAM**
		scant 1½ cups all-purpose flour, plus extra for dusting	7 oz/200 g semisweet chocolate, broken into small pieces
serves 4		scant ½ cup butter, diced, plus extra for greasing	2 eggs, separated
			scant ½ cup milk
30 minutes + 30 minutes to rest		½ cup confectioner's sugar, sifted	½ cup superfine sugar
		finely grated zest of 1 orange	8 amaretti biscuits, crushed
		1 egg yolk, beaten	1 tbsp orange liqueur
		3 tbsp milk	1 tbsp finely grated orange zest
1 hour			½ cup heavy cream
			finely grated orange zest, to decorate

To make the pie dough, sift the flour into a bowl. Rub in the butter. Mix in the sugar, orange zest, egg yolk, and milk. Knead briefly on a lightly floured counter, then let rest for 30 minutes. Preheat the oven to 350°F/180°C. Grease a 9-inch/23-cm tart pan with butter. Roll out two-thirds of the dough to a thickness of ¼ inch/5 mm and use it to line the bottom and sides of the tin.

To make the filling, melt the chocolate in a heatproof bowl over a pan of simmering water. Beat in the egg yolks, then the milk. Remove from the heat. In a separate bowl, whisk the egg whites until stiff, then stir in the sugar. Fold the egg whites into the chocolate, then stir in the biscuits. Spoon into the tart shell. Roll out the remaining dough, cut into strips, and use to form a lattice over the tart. Bake for 1 hour. To make the orange cream, beat together the orange liqueur, orange zest and cream. Remove the tart from the oven, decorate with orange zest, and serve with the orange cream.

lemon tart

		ingredients	
easy		**PIE DOUGH**	**FILLING**
		scant 1 ½ cups all-purpose flour, plus	4 eggs
		extra for dusting	1 ¼ cups superfine sugar
serves 4		3 tbsp ground almonds	juice and finely grated zest of 2 lemons
		scant ½ cup butter, diced, plus extra	⅔ cup heavy cream
		for greasing	
20 minutes + 1 ¼ hours to rest/cool		scant ½ cup confectioner's	mascarpone or crème fraîche, to serve
		sugar, sifted	
		finely grated zest of 1 lemon	
1 hour		1 egg yolk, beaten	
		3 tbsp milk	

To make the pie dough, sift the flour into a bowl. Mix in the almonds, then rub in the butter. Mix in the confectioner's sugar, lemon zest, egg yolk, and milk. Knead briefly on a lightly floured counter, then let rest for 30 minutes.

Preheat the oven to 350°F/180°C. Grease a 9-inch/23-cm tart pan with butter. Roll out the dough to a thickness of ¼ inch/5 mm and use to line the bottom and sides of the pan. Prick all over the bottom with a fork, line with baking parchment and fill with baking beans. Bake for 15 minutes. Remove from the oven. Lower the temperature to 300°F/150°C.

To make the filling, break the eggs into a bowl. Whisk in the sugar, then the lemon juice and zest and cream. Spoon into the tart shell and bake for 45 minutes. Remove from the oven and let cool for 45 minutes. Serve with mascarpone or crème fraîche.

peach & strawberry tart

		ingredients
easy		
	PIE DOUGH	**FILLING**
serves 4	scant 1 1/2 cups all-purpose flour, plus	3/4 cup heavy cream
	extra for dusting	4 tbsp confectioner's sugar
	scant 1/2 cup butter, diced, plus extra	1 tbsp peach liqueur
20 minutes +	for greasing	4 tbsp strawberry preserve
1 1/4 hours to	scant 1/2 cup confectioner's	2 peaches, pitted and sliced
rest/cool	sugar, sifted	3 1/2 oz/100 g strawberries, hulled
	finely grated zest of 1 orange	and sliced
	1 egg yolk, beaten	confectioner's sugar, to dust
15 minutes	3 tbsp milk	whipped cream, to serve

To make the dough, sift the flour into a bowl. Rub in the butter, then mix in the sugar, orange zest, egg yolk, and milk. Knead briefly on a lightly floured counter, then let rest for 30 minutes. Preheat the oven to 350°F/180°C. Grease a 9-inch/23-cm tart pan with butter. Roll out the dough to a thickness of 1/4 inch/5 mm and use to line the bottom and sides of the tin. Prick the bottom with a fork, line with baking parchment, and fill with baking beans. Bake for 15 minutes. Remove from the oven and set aside.

To make the filling, put the cream into a bowl and beat in the confectioner's sugar. Stir in the peach liqueur. Spread the bottom of the pastry shell with strawberry preserve, then spoon in the cream filling. Arrange the sliced peaches and strawberries over the top, then cover with plastic wrap and refrigerate for 45 minutes. Remove from the refrigerator, dust with confectioner's sugar, and serve with whipped cream.

spiced apple tart

	ingredients	
easy	**PIE DOUGH**	**FILLING**
	scant 1½ cups all-purpose flour, plus extra for dusting	3 medium tart cooking apples
		2 tbsp lemon juice
serves 4	scant ½ cup butter, diced, plus extra for greasing	finely grated zest of 1 lemon
		⅔ cup honey
20 minutes + 30 minutes to rest	scant ½ cup confectioner's sugar, sifted	3 cups fresh white or whole-wheat breadcrumbs
	finely grated zest of 1 lemon	1 tsp ground allspice
	1 egg yolk, beaten	pinch of ground nutmeg
	3 tbsp milk	
35 minutes		whipped cream, to serve

To make the pie dough, sift the flour into a bowl. Rub in the butter. Mix in the confectioner's sugar, lemon zest, egg yolk, and milk. Knead briefly on a lightly floured counter. Let rest for 30 minutes.

Preheat the oven to 400°F/200°C. Grease an 8-inch/20-cm tart pan with butter. Roll out the dough to a thickness of ¼ inch/5 mm and use to line the bottom and sides of the tart pan.

To make the filling, core 2 apples and grate them into a bowl. Add 1 tablespoon of lemon juice and all the lemon zest, along with the honey, breadcrumbs, and allspice. Mix together well. Spoon evenly into the tart shell. Core and slice the remaining apple, and use to decorate the top of the tart. Brush the apple slices with lemon juice, then sprinkle over the nutmeg. Bake in the preheated oven for 35 minutes, or until firm. Remove from the oven and serve with whipped cream.

hot
desserts

This chapter presents a truly spectacular selection of hot desserts for you to try, from delicious Pear Crêpes with Chocolate Sauce to a mouthwatering Blueberry Clafoutis. For fruit-lovers everywhere, these desserts are a veritable feast: pears, blueberries, raspberries, blackberries, strawberries, nectarines, pineapples, plums, peaches, bananas, and apricots all vie for your attention. And for those who love the combination of chocolate and cream, the Profiteroles simply cannot be missed.

pear crêpes
with chocolate sauce

		ingredients	
easy		CRÊPES	FILLING
		scant 1 cup all-purpose flour	9 oz/250 g sweet pears
serves 4		pinch of salt	8 cloves
		3 eggs	3 tbsp currants
		generous 1 cup milk	pinch of ground allspice
15 minutes + 30 minutes to chill		2 tbsp lemon oil or vegetable oil	SAUCE
			4½ oz/125 g semisweet chocolate, broken into small pieces
35 minutes			2½ tbsp butter
			6 tbsp water

To make the crêpes, sift the flour and salt into a bowl. Whisk in the eggs and milk to make a batter. Cover with plastic wrap and chill for 30 minutes. Heat a little oil in a skillet until hot. Add a large spoonful of the batter and cook over high heat until golden, then turn over and cook briefly on the other side. Cook the other crêpes in the same way, stacking them on a plate. Preheat the oven to 325°F/160°C.

To make the filling, bring a pan of water to a boil. Peel and slice the pears; add to the pan with the cloves and currants. Lower the heat and simmer for 5 minutes. Remove from the heat, drain, and discard the cloves. Let cool a little. Oil an ovenproof dish. Stir the allspice into the fruit; divide between the crêpes. Fold the crêpes into triangles or roll into horns. Arrange in the dish and bake for 15 minutes. To make the sauce, melt the chocolate and butter with the water in a small pan, stirring. Serve the crêpes with the sauce.

warm fruit nests

		ingredients	
easy	2–3 tbsp lemon oil	3 tbsp superfine sugar	
	8 sheets of frozen phyllo pastry, thawed	1 tsp ground allspice	
serves 4	9 oz/250 g blueberries	sprigs of fresh mint, to decorate	
	9 oz/250 g raspberries	heavy cream, to serve	
15–20 minutes	9 oz/250 g blackberries		
10 minutes			

Preheat the oven to 350°F/180°C. Brush 4 small muffin pans with oil. Cut the phyllo pastry into 16 squares measuring about 12 cm/ 4½ inches across. Brush each square with oil and use to line the muffin pans. Place 4 sheets in each pan, staggering them so that the overhanging corners make a decorative star shape. Transfer to a cookie sheet and bake in the preheated oven for 7–8 minutes, until golden. Remove from the oven and set aside.

Meanwhile, warm the fruit in a pan with the superfine sugar and allspice over medium heat until simmering. Lower the heat and continue simmering, stirring, for 10 minutes. Remove from the heat and drain. Using a perforated spoon, divide the warm fruit between the tartlet shells. Garnish with sprigs of fresh mint and serve warm with heavy cream.

fruit skewers

		ingredients	
very easy		**SKEWERS**	**CHOCOLATE ALMOND SAUCE**
		6 tbsp brown sugar	4¹/₂ oz/125 g semisweet chocolate,
		pinch of ground allspice	broken into small pieces
serves 4		8 whole strawberries, hulled	2¹/₂ tbsp butter
		3 nectarines, pitted and cut into	6 tbsp water
		bite-size chunks	1 tbsp almond liqueur, such as
15–20 minutes		14 oz/400 g canned pineapple	Amaretto
		chunks, drained	
		4 plums, pitted and cut into	chopped mixed nuts, to decorate
10–12 minutes		bite-size chunks	
		6 tbsp butter, melted	

Combine the sugar and allspice and spread out on a large plate. Thread the whole strawberries onto metal skewers, alternating with the chunks of nectarine, pineapple, and plum. When the skewers are full (leave a small space at either end), brush them with melted butter, then turn them in the sugar until lightly coated. Transfer to a barbecue grill or a preheated broiler and cook, turning occasionally, for 8–10 minutes.

To make the sauce, gently melt the chocolate and butter with the water together in a small pan, stirring constantly, until smooth. Stir in the almond liqueur. Remove the skewers from the heat. Divide between individual plates, decorate with chopped mixed nuts, and serve hot with the chocolate almond sauce.

stuffed pears

		ingredients	
very easy	scant ½ cup honey	4 large sweet pears	
	½ cup maple syrup	4 tbsp sweet mincemeat	
serves 4	1 tbsp lemon juice		
	4 tbsp water	whipped cream, to serve	
	½ tsp ground cinnamon		
15 minutes			
1¼ hours			

Preheat the oven to 325°F/160°C. Gently warm the honey, maple syrup, lemon juice, water, and cinnamon, stir well and pour into a glass pitcher. Core and peel the pears. Using a sharp knife, cut a small slice off the bottom of each pear so that they will stand up straight. Spoon some mincemeat into the centers, then stand them in an ovenproof dish. Pour the syrup mixture over the top, then transfer to the preheated oven. Bake, uncovered, for about 1¼ hours, basting with the syrup from time to time, until cooked right through.

Remove from the oven and transfer to individual serving plates. Serve warm, with generous spoonfuls of whipped cream.

profiteroles

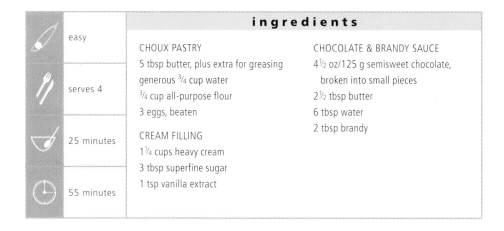

ingredients

easy

serves 4

25 minutes

55 minutes

CHOUX PASTRY
5 tbsp butter, plus extra for greasing
generous ¾ cup water
¾ cup all-purpose flour
3 eggs, beaten

CREAM FILLING
1¼ cups heavy cream
3 tbsp superfine sugar
1 tsp vanilla extract

CHOCOLATE & BRANDY SAUCE
4½ oz/125 g semisweet chocolate,
  broken into small pieces
2½ tbsp butter
6 tbsp water
2 tbsp brandy

Preheat the oven to 400°F/200°C. Grease a large cookie sheet with butter. To make the pastry, put the water and butter into a pan and bring to a boil. Meanwhile, sift the flour into a bowl. Remove the pan from the heat and beat in the flour until smooth. Cool for 5 minutes. Beat in enough of the eggs to give the mixture a soft, dropping consistency. Transfer into a pastry bag fitted with a ½-inch/1-cm plain tip. Pipe small balls onto the cookie sheet. Bake for 25 minutes. Remove from the oven. Pierce each ball with a skewer to let steam escape.

To make the filling, whip together the cream, sugar, and vanilla extract. Cut the pastry balls almost in half, then fill with cream.

To make the sauce, gently melt the chocolate, butter, and water together in a small pan, stirring, until smooth. Stir in the brandy. Pile the profiteroles into individual serving dishes or into a pyramid on a raised cake stand. Pour over the sauce and serve.

fruit crêpes

		ingredients	
easy		CRÊPES	2 nectarines, pitted and cut into
		scant 1 cup all-purpose flour	small pieces
		pinch of salt	1 mango, peeled, pitted, and cut into
serves 4		2 eggs	small pieces
		1¼ cups milk	3 kiwifruits, peeled and cut into
15–20		2–3 tbsp vegetable oil	small pieces
minutes +			2 tbsp maple syrup
30 minutes		FILLING	
to chill		1 banana	confectioner's sugar, to dust
15 minutes		1 tbsp lemon juice	
			whipped cream, to serve

To make the crêpes, sift the flour and salt into a bowl. Whisk in the eggs and milk. Cover with plastic wrap and chill for 30 minutes.

To make the filling, peel and slice the banana and put into a large bowl. Pour over the lemon juice and stir gently until coated. Add the nectarines, mango, kiwifruits, and maple syrup, and stir together gently until mixed.

Heat a little oil in a skillet until hot. Remove the crêpe batter from the refrigerator and add a large spoonful to the pan. Cook over high heat until golden, then turn over and cook briefly on the other side. Remove from the pan and keep warm. Cook the other crêpes in the same way, stacking them on a plate. Keep warm. Divide the fruit filling between the crêpes and fold into triangles or roll into horns. Dust with confectioner's sugar and serve with whipped cream.

baked peaches with orange liqueur cream

very easy		
serves 4		
20 minutes		
30 minutes		

ingredients

$^1/_3$ cup shelled pistachios, finely
  chopped
$^1/_3$ cup toasted hazelnuts,
  finely chopped
1 tbsp grated orange zest
1 tbsp brown sugar
pinch of ground allspice
4 large, ripe (but firm) peaches
1 tbsp unsalted butter

HONEY SYRUP
$^1/_2$ cup water
1 tbsp honey
2 tsp freshly squeezed orange juice
generous $^3/_4$ cup superfine sugar
pinch of ground allspice

ORANGE LIQUEUR CREAM
1 tbsp finely grated orange zest
$^1/_2$ cup heavy cream
1 tbsp orange liqueur

Preheat the oven to 350°F/180°C. Put the nuts, orange zest, brown sugar, and allspice into a mixing bowl and stir together well. Halve the peaches and remove the pits. Remove a little of the flesh in the center of each peach, chop into pieces, and stir into the nut mixture. Place a little of the mixture into the hollow in each peach. Transfer the peaches to an ovenproof dish and dot with butter. Bake in the preheated oven for 30 minutes.

About halfway through the cooking time, make the honey syrup. Put the water, honey, orange juice, superfine sugar, and allspice into a pan and bring to a boil, stirring constantly. Lower the heat and simmer, without stirring, for about 15 minutes.

To make the orange liqueur cream, put the orange zest and cream into a bowl and beat together, then stir in the liqueur. Remove the peaches from the oven and divide between serving dishes. Pour over the honey syrup and serve with the orange liqueur cream.

toffee bananas

		ingredients	
easy		½ cup self-rising flour	CARAMEL
		1 egg, beaten	generous ½ cup superfine sugar
serves 4		5 tbsp iced water	4 tbsp iced water, plus an extra bowl
		4 large, ripe bananas	of iced water for setting
		3 tbsp lemon juice	2 tbsp sesame seeds
20 minutes		2 tbsp rice flour	
		vegetable oil, for deep-frying	
15–20 minutes			

Sift the flour into a bowl. Make a well in the center, add the egg and 5 tablespoons of the iced water, and beat from the center outwards, until combined into a smooth batter. Peel the bananas and cut into 2-inch/5-cm pieces. Gently shape them into balls with your hands. Brush with lemon juice to prevent discoloration, then roll them in rice flour until coated. Pour oil into a pan to a depth of 2½ inches/6 cm and preheat to 375°F/190°C. Coat the balls in the batter, and cook in batches in the hot oil for about 2 minutes each, until golden. Lift them out and drain on paper towels.

To make the caramel, put the sugar into a small pan over low heat. Add 4 tablespoons of iced water and heat, stirring, until the sugar dissolves. Simmer for 5 minutes, remove from the heat, and stir in the sesame seeds. Toss the banana balls in the caramel, scoop them out, and drop into the bowl of iced water to set. Lift them out and divide between individual serving bowls. Serve hot.

blueberry clafoutis

		ingredients
very easy	2 tbsp butter, plus extra for greasing	$\frac{1}{2}$ tsp ground cinnamon
	scant $\frac{2}{3}$ cup superfine sugar	1 lb/450 g blueberries
serves 4	3 eggs	
	scant $\frac{1}{2}$ cup all-purpose flour	confectioner's sugar, to dust
	generous 1 cup light cream	
15 minutes		light cream, to serve
30 minutes		

Preheat the oven to 350°F/180°C. Grease a 4-cup ovenproof dish with butter.

Put the remaining butter into a bowl with the sugar, and cream together until fluffy. Add the eggs and beat together well. Mix in the flour, then gradually stir in the cream, followed by the cinnamon. Continue to stir until smooth.

Arrange the blueberries evenly across the bottom of the prepared dish, then pour over the cream batter. Transfer to the preheated oven and bake for about 30 minutes, or until puffed and golden. Remove from the oven, dust with confectioner's sugar, and serve with light cream.

apricot crumble

		ingredients
very easy		generous ½ cup butter, plus extra for greasing scant 1 cup brown sugar 1 lb 2 oz/500 g fresh apricots, pitted and sliced 1 tsp ground cinnamon	scant 1¼ cups whole-wheat flour ⅓ cup hazelnuts, toasted and finely chopped clotted cream, to serve
serves 4			
15 minutes			
30–35 minutes			

Preheat the oven to 400°F/200°C. Grease a 5-cup ovenproof dish with butter.

Put 3 tablespoons of the butter into a pan, then add all but 2 tablespoons of the sugar, and melt together, stirring, over low heat. Add the apricots and cinnamon, cover the pan, and simmer for 5 minutes.

Meanwhile, put the flour into a bowl and rub in the remaining butter. Stir in the remaining sugar, then the hazelnuts. Remove the fruit from the heat and arrange in the bottom of the prepared dish. Sprinkle the crumble topping evenly over the fruit until it is covered all over. Transfer to the preheated oven and bake for about 25 minutes, until golden. Remove from the oven and serve hot with clotted cream.

cold
desserts

Cold desserts are delightful, and they can often be prepared in advance, leaving you more time for other things. If you are entertaining, this chapter presents an exciting selection of table centerpieces, from a rich Chocolate & Cherry Tiramisù to a spectacular Mixed Fruit Pavlova. The Cherry Baskets will look very impressive on your table, and so will the Blueberry Coeur à la Crème, while elegant Rose Petal Ice Cream will intrigue your guests. If you would prefer a lighter finish to your meal, try one of the refreshing sherbets in this section.

raspberry meringue

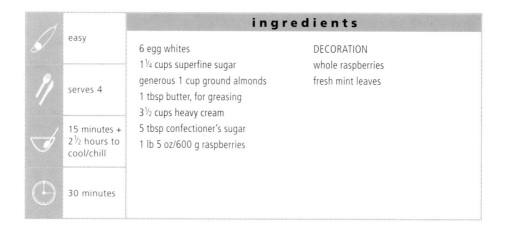

easy	
serves 4	
15 minutes + 2½ hours to cool/chill	
30 minutes	

ingredients

6 egg whites
1¼ cups superfine sugar
generous 1 cup ground almonds
1 tbsp butter, for greasing
3½ cups heavy cream
5 tbsp confectioner's sugar
1 lb 5 oz/600 g raspberries

DECORATION
whole raspberries
fresh mint leaves

Preheat the oven to 300°F/150°C. Put the egg whites into a bowl and whisk until stiff peaks form. Gradually whisk in the superfine sugar, then fold in the almonds.

Grease two 8-inch/20-cm cake pans with butter and line with waxed paper. Divide the meringue mixture between the pans and level the surfaces. Transfer to the preheated oven and bake for 30 minutes. Remove from the oven. Let cool on a wire rack.

Put the cream into a bowl, add the confectioner's sugar, and whip until soft peaks form. Put one of the baked meringues onto a cake stand or serving plate and spread over a generous layer of the sugared cream. Top with a layer of raspberries, then cover with the remaining meringue. Spread the remaining cream evenly over the top of the cake, and chill in the refrigerator for at least 2 hours.

Remove from the refrigerator, decorate with raspberries and fresh mint leaves, and serve.

chocolate & cherry tiramisù

		ingredients	
very easy	generous ¾ cup strong black coffee, cooled to room temperature	3 tbsp confectioner's sugar
serves 4	6 tbsp cherry brandy 16 trifle sponges 1¼ mascarpone	9½ oz/275 g sweet cherries, halved and pitted 2¼ oz/60 g chocolate, curls or grated
20 minutes + 2 hours to chill	1¼ cups heavy cream, lightly whipped	whole cherries, to decorate
—		

Pour the cooled coffee into a pitcher and stir in the cherry brandy. Put half of the trifle sponges into the bottom of a serving dish, then pour over half of the coffee mixture.

Put the mascarpone into a separate bowl along with the cream and sugar, and mix together well. Spread half of the mascarpone mixture over the coffee-soaked trifle sponges, then top with half of the cherries. Arrange the remaining trifle sponges on top. Pour over the remaining coffee mixture and top with the remaining cherries. Finish with a layer of mascarpone mixture. Scatter over the grated chocolate, cover with plastic wrap, and chill in the refrigerator for at least 2 hours.

Remove from the refrigerator, decorate with cherries, and serve.

pineapple cheesecake

	ingredients	
extremely easy	4 oz/115 g graham crackers, finely crushed	generous 1½ cups creamed cottage cheese
serves 4	4 tbsp butter, melted, plus extra for greasing	⅔ cup heavy cream, whipped
	½ cup superfine sugar	14 oz/400 g canned pineapple slices, drained and halved
20 minutes + 4 hours to chill	juice of 1 lemon	
	2 tbsp grated lemon zest	pinch of ground nutmeg, to decorate (optional)
—	generous 1½ cups cream cheese	

Put the crushed crackers into a large bowl and mix in the melted butter. Grease an 8-inch/20-cm loose-bottomed cake pan with butter, then press the cracker mixture evenly over the bottom.

Put the sugar into a separate bowl and stir in the lemon juice and the lemon zest. Add the cheeses and beat until thoroughly combined. Fold in the cream. Spread the cream mixture evenly over the cracker layer. Cover with plastic wrap and place in the refrigerator to chill for at least 4 hours.

Remove the cheesecake from the refrigerator, turn out onto a serving platter, and spread the pineapple slices over the top. Sprinkle over a little ground nutmeg, if using. Serve immediately.

mixed fruit pavlova

		ingredients	
easy		6 egg whites	9 oz/250 g strawberries, hulled
		pinch of cream of tartar	and sliced
serves 4		pinch of salt	3 ripe peaches, sliced
		1½ cups superfine sugar	1 ripe mango, peeled and sliced
		scant 2½ cups heavy cream	2 tbsp orange liqueur, such
30 minutes + 30 minutes to cool		1 tsp vanilla extract	as Cointreau
		2 kiwifruits, peeled and sliced	
			fresh mint leaves, to decorate
3 hours			

Preheat the oven to 225°F/110°C. Line 3 cookie sheets with baking parchment, then draw an 8½-inch/22-cm circle in the center of each one. Beat the egg whites into stiff peaks. Mix in the cream of tartar and salt. Gradually add 1 cup of sugar. Beat for 2 minutes until glossy. Fill a pastry bag with the mixture and use it to fill each circle, making them slightly domed in the center. Bake for 3 hours. Remove from the oven and let cool.

Whip together the cream and vanilla extract with all but 2 tablespoons of the remaining sugar. Put the fruit into a separate bowl and stir in the liqueur. Put one meringue circle onto a serving plate, then spread over one-third of the sugared cream. Spread over one-third of the fruit, then top with a meringue. Spread over another third of cream, then another third of fruit. Top with the last meringue. Spread over the remaining cream, followed by the remaining fruit. Decorate with mint leaves and serve.

sherry trifle

		ingredients	
easy		FRUIT LAYER	CUSTARD LAYER
		6 trifle sponge cakes	generous 1 cup heavy cream
		2 tbsp strawberry preserve	1 tsp vanilla extract
serves 4		6 large strawberries, hulled and sliced	3 egg yolks
		2 bananas, peeled and sliced	4 tbsp superfine sugar
15 minutes + 4½ hours to cool/chill		14 oz/400 g canned sliced peaches, drained	TOPPING
			1¼ cups heavy cream
		6 tbsp sherry	2 tbsp superfine sugar
5 minutes			toasted, chopped mixed nuts, to decorate

To make the fruit layer, spread the sponge cakes with preserve, cut into bite-size pieces, and arrange in the bottom of a glass serving bowl. Scatter over the fruit, pour over the sherry, and set aside.

To make the custard, put the cream and vanilla extract into a pan and bring almost to a boil over a low heat. Meanwhile, put the egg yolks and sugar into a bowl and whisk together well. Remove the cream from the heat and gradually stir into the egg mixture. Return the mixture to the pan and warm over low heat, stirring, until thickened. Remove the custard from the heat and let cool for 30 minutes, then pour it evenly over the fruit layer. Cover with plastic wrap and chill for 2½ hours.

Remove the trifle from the refrigerator. To make the topping, whip together the cream and sugar, then spread it evenly over the custard layer. Scatter over the toasted chopped nuts, then cover again with plastic wrap and chill for a further 1½ hours. Serve chilled.

cherry baskets

easy

serves 4

25 minutes
+ 1 hour
to set

20 minutes

BASKETS
3 tbsp unsalted butter, plus extra
  for greasing
3 tbsp superfine sugar
4 tbsp corn syrup
$\frac{1}{2}$ tsp ground allspice
1 tsp almond extract
1 tbsp cherry brandy
5 tbsp all-purpose flour

FILLING
10$\frac{1}{2}$ oz/300 g cherries, pitted
1 tbsp cherry brandy
$\frac{2}{3}$ cup heavy cream, whipped

GLAZE
5$\frac{1}{2}$ oz/150 g redcurrant jelly
1 tbsp water

To make the baskets, put the butter, sugar, and syrup into a pan and stir over medium heat until melted. Simmer for 3 minutes, then remove from the heat. Stir in the spice, almond extract, and brandy. Gradually mix in the flour, and set aside for 10 minutes.

Preheat the oven to 350°F/180°C. Grease a large cookie sheet with butter. Drop enough of the mixture onto the sheet to make 4 circles, 4 inches/10 cm in diameter, leaving space for each of them to expand. Shape the remaining mixture into 4 "handles" and lay them separately on the baking sheet. Bake for 15 minutes, or until golden. Remove from the oven, then mold the basket shapes over the bottoms of 4 cups. Remove the baskets, add the handles, and press to secure. Let stand for 1 hour to set.

To make the filling, mix the cherries with the brandy. Spoon cream into each basket and top with the cherries. To glaze, melt the redcurrant jelly with the water and brush over the cherries. Serve.

raspberry brûlées

		ingredients	
	very easy	9 oz/250 g raspberries	1 tsp vanilla extract
		1 tbsp lemon juice	6 tbsp superfine sugar
	serves 4	2 tbsp raspberry preserve	
		½ cup crème fraîche or mascarpone	whole raspberries, to decorate
		½ cup heavy cream, lightly whipped	
	10 minutes		
	7–8 minutes		

Put the raspberries and lemon juice into a pan and stir over low heat for about 5 minutes until they start to soften. Remove from the heat, stir in the preserve, then divide between 4 ramekins.

Preheat the broiler to hot. In a bowl, mix together the crème fraîche, cream, and vanilla. Spoon the mixture over the raspberries and level the surfaces. Sprinkle the superfine sugar over the top, allowing 1½ tablespoons per ramekin. Cook under the preheated broiler, as close to the flames or element as possible, for 2–3 minutes, until the sugar caramelizes. Remove from the broiler, decorate with whole raspberries, and serve immediately. Alternatively, to serve chilled, let cool to room temperature, then cover with plastic wrap and place in the refrigerator to chill for 3–4 hours.

rich chocolate mousses

easy	
serves 4	
10 minutes + 4 hours to chill	
5 minutes	

ingredients

10½ oz/300 g semisweet chocolate (at least 70% cocoa solids)
1½ tbsp unsalted butter

1 tbsp brandy
4 eggs, separated

unsweetened cocoa, to dust

Break the chocolate into small pieces and put it into a heatproof bowl over a pan of simmering water. Add the butter and melt with the chocolate, stirring, until smooth. Remove from the heat, stir in the brandy, and let cool a little. Add the egg yolks and beat until smooth.

In a separate bowl, whisk the egg whites until stiff peaks have formed, then fold them into the chocolate mixture. Divide 4 stainless steel cooking rings between 4 small serving plates, then spoon the mixture into each ring and level the surfaces. Transfer to the refrigerator and chill for at least 4 hours until set.

Remove the mousses from the refrigerator and discard the cooking rings. Dust with unsweetened cocoa and serve.

blueberry coeur à la crème

		ingredients	
very easy	scant 1 cup cream cheese	BLUEBERRY COULIS	
	scant 1 cup crème fraîche	7 oz/200 g blueberries	
	or mascarpone cheese	juice of ½ lemon	
serves 4	2 egg whites, whisked	1 tbsp confectioners' sugar	
	2 tbsp superfine sugar		
	1 tsp vanilla extract	whole blueberries, to decorate	
20 minutes + 2 hours to chill			
—			

Put the cream cheese, crème fraîche, and whisked egg whites into a bowl and mix well. Stir in the superfine sugar and vanilla extract. Line a large coeur à la crème mold with cheesecloth, spoon in the cheese mixture, and level the surface. Fold the edges of the cheesecloth over the top.

Place a wire rack over a tray, then place the mold on the wire rack. Transfer to the refrigerator to drain and chill for at least 2 hours.

To make the coulis, put the blueberries into a food processor and process into a paste, then press through a strainer into a bowl. Stir in the lemon juice and confectioners' sugar, then cover with plastic wrap and chill until required.

To serve, carefully turn out the cheese from the mold and discard the cheesecloth. Decorate with whole blueberries and serve with the blueberry coulis.

banana splits

		ingredients	
easy		4 bananas	CHOCOLATE RUM SAUCE
			4 1/2 oz/125 g semisweet chocolate,
		VANILLA ICE CREAM	broken into small pieces
serves 4		1 1/4 cups milk	2 1/2 tbsp butter
		1 tsp vanilla extract	6 tbsp water
		3 egg yolks	1 tbsp rum
1 3/4–4 hours		1/2 cup superfine sugar	
		1 1/4 cups heavy cream, whipped	6 tbsp chopped mixed nuts,
			to decorate
5–10 minutes			

To make the ice cream, heat the milk and vanilla extract in a pan until almost boiling. In a bowl, beat together the egg yolks and sugar. Remove the milk from the heat and stir a little into the egg mixture. Transfer the mixture to the pan. Stir over low heat until thick. Do not boil. Remove from the heat. Cool for 30 minutes, fold in the cream, cover with plastic wrap, and chill for 1 hour. Transfer into an ice cream maker and process for 15 minutes. Alternatively, transfer into a freezerproof container and freeze for 1 hour, then place in a bowl and beat to break up the ice crystals. Put back in the container and freeze for 30 minutes. Repeat twice more, freezing for 30 minutes and whisking each time.

To make the sauce, melt the chocolate and butter with the water together in a pan, stirring. Remove from the heat and stir in the rum. Peel the bananas, slice them lengthwise, and arrange on 4 serving dishes. Top with ice cream and nuts and serve with the sauce.

rose petal ice cream

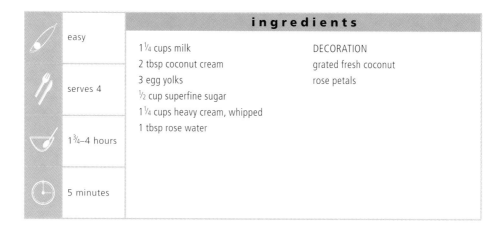

	ingredients	
easy	1 1/4 cups milk	DECORATION
	2 tbsp coconut cream	grated fresh coconut
	3 egg yolks	rose petals
serves 4	1/2 cup superfine sugar	
	1 1/4 cups heavy cream, whipped	
	1 tbsp rose water	
1 3/4–4 hours		
5 minutes		

Pour the milk into a pan, stir in the coconut cream, and heat gently until almost boiling. In a bowl, beat together the egg yolks and sugar. Remove the milk from the heat and stir a little into the egg mixture. Transfer the mixture to the pan and stir over low heat until thickened and smooth. Do not let it boil. Remove from the heat and let cool for 30 minutes. Fold in the cream, then stir in the rose water. Cover with plastic wrap and chill for 1 hour.

Remove from the refrigerator. Transfer into an ice cream maker and process for 15 minutes. Alternatively, transfer into a freezerproof container and freeze for 1 hour, then place in a bowl and beat to break up the ice crystals. Put back in the container and freeze for 30 minutes. Repeat twice more, freezing for 30 minutes and whisking each time. Store in the freezer until required.

Remove from the freezer and scoop into serving dishes. Scatter over the grated coconut and rose petals and serve immediately.

peach & banana sherbet

		ingredients
very easy	4 large peaches	fresh mint leaves, to decorate
serves 4	2 bananas	
20 minutes + 4 hours to freeze	1 tbsp peach brandy	
—		

Peel and stone the peaches, then cut the flesh into small chunks. Arrange them in a single layer on a cookie tray. Peel and slice the bananas and arrange in a single layer on another cookie tray. Transfer the trays to the freezer and freeze for 4 hours.

Remove the frozen peaches and bananas from the freezer and transfer into a food processor. Pour in the peach brandy and process until the mixture is smooth. The sherbet can then be stored in the freezer until required.

When required, scoop the sherbet into serving bowls, decorate with fresh mint leaves, and serve immediately.

orange sherbet

		ingredients	
easy		generous 2 cups water	1 tbsp orange conserve or marmalade
		1 cup superfine sugar	
serves 4		4 large oranges	candied orange peel, to decorate
1¾–4 hours			
5 minutes			

Heat the water and sugar in a pan over low heat, stirring, until the sugar has dissolved. Bring to a boil, then continue to boil without stirring for 2 minutes. Remove from the heat and pour the mixture into a heatproof, nonmetallic (glass or ceramic) bowl, which will not react with acid. Let cool to room temperature.

Grate the zest from 2 of the oranges, then extract the juice from all 4. Mix the juice, zest, and orange conserve in a bowl, then stir into the sugar syrup. Cover with plastic wrap and chill for 1 hour. Transfer into an ice cream maker and process for 15 minutes. Alternatively, transfer into a freezerproof container and freeze for 1 hour, then place in a bowl and beat to break up the ice crystals. Put back in the container and freeze for 30 minutes. Repeat twice more, freezing for 30 minutes and whisking each time. Store in the freezer until required.

Remove from the freezer and scoop into serving bowls. Decorate with candied orange peel and serve.

index

apples
    Eve's bake 18
    tart 44
    upside-down cake 24
apricot crumble 66

baked peaches with orange
liqueur cream 60
bakewell tart 36
bananas
    banoffee pie 32
    fruit crêpes 58
    peach sorbet 92
    sherry trifle 78
    splits 88
    toffee 62
banoffee pie 32
blueberries
    clafoutis 64
    coeur à la crème 86
    coulis 86
bread & butter dessert 22
brûlées 82

cakes
    apple upside-down 24
    chocolate cherry layer 26
cheesecake 74
cherry baskets 80
chocolate
    cherry layer cake 26
    & cherry tiramisù 72
    dessert 10
    desserts 10
    mousses 84
    orange tart 38
    sauces 10, 48, 52, 56, 88
cold desserts 68–94
coulis 86
creamy rice dessert 16
crêpes
    fruit 58
    pear 48
crumble 66

Eve's apple bake 18

forest fruit pie 30
fruit
    nests 50
    crêpes 58
    pavlova 76
    pie 30
    skewers 52

honey syrup 60
hot desserts 12, 16, 22, 46–66
hot syrup sponge 12

ice cream
    banana splits 88
    rose petal 90
individual chocolate desserts 10

layer cake 26
lemons
    meringue pie 34
    tart 40

meringue
    lemon 34
    raspberry 70
mixed fruit pavlova 76
mousses 84

oranges
    cream 38
    sherbet 94

pavlova 76
peaches
    & banana sherbet 92
    with orange liqueur cream 60
    pavlova 76
    & strawberry tart 42
pears
    crêpes with chocolate sauce 48
    stuffed 54
pies
    banoffee 32
    forest fruit 30
    lemon meringue 34
pineapple cheesecake 74
profiteroles 56
puddings
    roly poly 14
    summer 20

raspberries
    brûlées 82
    meringue 70
rice dessert 16
rich chocolate mousses 84
roly poly pudding 14
rose petal ice cream 90

sauces
    chocolate 10, 48
    chocolate almond 52
    chocolate and brandy 56
    chocolate rum 88
    orange liqueur cream 60
    sticky toffee 8
sherbets
    orange 94
    peach & banana 92
sherry trifle 78
spiced apple tart 44
sponges
    hot syrup 12
    sticky toffee 8
sticky toffee sponge 8
strawberries
    pavlova 76
    peach tart 42
    sherry trifle 78
stuffed pears 54
summer pudding 20
syrup sponge 12

tarts
    bakewell 36
    chocolate orange 38
    lemon 40
    peach & strawberry 42
    spiced apple 44
tiramisù 72
toffee
    bananas 62
    banoffee pie 32
    pudding 8
trifle 78

warm fruit nests 50